SCOTTISH SYMPHONY

SCOTTISH SYMPHONY

Photographs by Michael Ruetz

Introduction by David Attenborough

Little, Brown and Company   Boston   Toronto   London

Reprinted in 1991 and published in Great Britain by Little, Brown and Company, 30 North End Road, London W14 0SH

ISBN 0-316-88887-7

A CIP catalogue record for this book is available from the British Library

Frontispiece: Eilean Donan Castle, Loch Duich, Ross and Cromarty, by Michael Ruetz

Designed by Carl Zahn

Printed and bound in Hong Kong by Dai Nippon Printing Company, Ltd.

Dedicated to the memory of the great American photographer Paul Strand and his work in the Hebrides

Introduction

by David Attenborough

Scotland is a separate land. The Scots are the first to make the point, especially to an Englishman such as myself. But they have no need to insist. The visitor, traveling north from England, rapidly realizes that he is crossing frontiers. If he has started from London, the journey may seem, to people from larger continents, to people from larger continents, to be absurdly short. Three hundred miles is quite enough to get him across the official Scottish border to towns where people's speech sounds so different that, in some parts and to some ears, it may be almost incomprehensible. Another hundred miles or so, and he will be entering the Highlands, the country where Michael Ruetz took most of these photographs, and there he may encounter not merely unfamiliar accents but a completely different language, Gaelic. A separate land indeed, and a separate people.

The hills, rising ahead, snow-covered in winter, hazy purple in summer, are more massive than anything he will have seen in England. They lack the jagged profiles of the Alps or the Rockies and, in comparison with such ranges, they are tiny, for only seven of them rise above 4,000 feet. But they are very much older. Indeed, it is precisely their antiquity that has given them their rounded shape and modest stature. They are a fragment, crumpled, cracked, and contorted, of the very first continent that appeared, 2,500 million years ago, like a curd on the surface of the cooling earth.

During the time of the dinosaurs, around 200 million years ago, they formed a separate island lying north of shallow tropical seas where rocks that were eventually to constitute the lands of England were being laid down as chalky mud.

Thirty million years ago, when those English lands had appeared, these mountains in the north were shaken by titanic earthquakes. Molten rock welled up beneath and solidified without breaking through the strata above. The stone blanket that covered it ultimately eroded away so that now granite can be seen on the rounded summits of the Cairngorms and on Ben Nevis, the highest of all British peaks. In the west, on the mainland and in the scatter of islands that stretches away into the Atlantic, molten lava spilled out through huge fissures in the ground. It cooled so rapidly that crystals had no time to form, with the result that, unlike granite, which contains separate minerals in crystals the size of gravel grains, it is a uniform, homogenous black stone, basalt. In Skye, this has eroded to form the Old Man of Storr and his teetering companions. On the island of Staffa, a thick flow has cooled so evenly that the contractions which accompany solidification spread uniformly through it, creating networks of long joints that divide the basalt into sheaves of hexagonal pillars.

More recently still, a mere 150,000 years ago, when the whole of the northern hemisphere was gripped by a series of Ice Ages, the Scottish hills formed the nucleus of an icecap from which glaciers flowed over the surrounding seas, across to Ireland and south over England almost as far as the valley of the Thames. They planed away the sides of the valleys, giving them a wide spacious spread, and they dug the deep beds that later were to be invaded by the sea and turned into lochs.

The world has warmed since then and the glaciers have melted. Today, there are no truly permanent snowfields in

Scotland, though there are a few remote north-facing corries on the flanks of the highest hills where snow stays long and may even survive through a cool summer. And on the flat bleak summits, the last British survivors of an Arctic flora still linger, tiny plants that otherwise are only found in any abundance at higher altitudes in the mountain ranges of Europe, or higher latitudes in the freezing lands of the Arctic.

Beneath these desolate summits, where the hillside can be blessedly warm in summer and a peaty soil lies between the boulders, there is still little vegetation much higher than your knees. But it was not always so. When human beings first came to settle here, the land was draped with great forests of birch, oak, and, in particular, pine. Scotland's true native pine is unlike all others growing elsewhere. It has short needles of a distinctive bottle green and its boughs are covered with a scaly bark that is a marvelous handsome red. When growing naturally, it is a tree of great individual character and beauty, vastly different from the regimented ranks of identical bolt-upright squads beloved by commercial foresters. One or two fragments of those ancient forests remain, but for the most part there are only a few isolated trees to be found, standing lonely and weather-beaten on the moors.

The destruction of the Scottish forests began a long time ago. When, during the Bronze Age, men erected standing stones like those of Callanish on the Isle of Lewis, they had already made a start by clearing much of the birch woods that then covered much of the island. That was about four thousand years ago. Two thousand years later, raiders in narrow ships from

Scandinavia, the Vikings, came sailing up the sea-lochs and repeatedly set fire to the forests to drive out the local people. When, at last, some degree of law was established over these wild lands and tribes, the felling of trees was continued and intensified, first to deny refuge to wolves and bears and bandits, then to provide timber to fuel the furnaces of iron smelters. Later still, men came up from the south with sheep and set fire to the forests, sometimes a whole valley at a time, just to create grazing for their flocks.

So today, the hillsides and moors of Scotland are treeless over vast areas. Heather and bracken stretch as far as the eye can see. The heather, which might, in the natural course of things, give way to taller bushes and eventually to trees, is carefully maintained and refreshed with regular burning, thus creating a supply of succulent young leaves that are the food of the red grouse. This bird is, arguably, the only species among all British birds that occurs nowhere else outside the British Isles, but, needless to say, it is not to preserve a unique ornithological possession that the moors are managed in this way. It is because the grouse, when driven by beaters, suddenly explodes into the air with a whirring erratic flight that, apparently, makes it an interesting challenge to marksmanship and therefore provides hunters with unique sport.

The Scottish Highlands have lost not only most of their trees but most of their people. The land was never very fertile, for the glaciers scraped most of the soil away. Even so, until the eighteenth century, the tribal chieftains managed to maintain small armies of tartan-clad, sword-wielding, cattle-keeping clansmen, together with their families. The chiefs, however, lost their power in the last large-scale fighting to take place on British soil, during the brutal battles of the Jacobite Revolutions. After those defeats, the English armies built roads through the Highlands, so that they could maintain military control over the clansmen. Eventually, those roads served not only for access but egress.

During the nineteenth century, many of the hereditary chieftains found life among their people in the Highlands arduous and uncomfortable. They abandoned their ancient territories and traveled south to the cities of the Scottish lowlands or beyond to England. Some retained the ownership of their lands and became absentee landlords, ignorant or careless of their tenants' needs and welfare. Others, worse, sold their land to men who, wishing to increase its profitability, concluded that the easiest way to do so was to evict the crofters who had lived there for many generations and replace them with sheep. Thus began the shameful Clearances, during which men, women, and children were turned off their crofts by the military, using clubs and bayonets where necessary. The Highlanders, sometimes by force, sometimes from despair, left their homeland. Some migrated to the coast and took to fishing. Many joined the Scots regiments that fought so valiantly in Britain's wars and sustained her Empire. Many more emigrated to build new homes and lives in distant parts of that Empire.

So the land in Michael Ruetz's evocative photographs appears, only too accurately, to be a largely empty one. He has caught the quintessential Highland images — fortified stone houses, three, four, or even five centuries old, small-windowed against the cold; stone walls standing strangely isolated in this hedgeless, treeless land; long roads running up wide glaciated valleys along which you can almost hear the tramp of alien armies that built them; and, predominantly, the mist-swathed profiles of these most ancient of hills. It is the very absence of people that offers to many of us who journey there from the crowded south a deep solace. Perhaps too, it is that absence that allows us to perceive so clearly the past history, stretching from centuries to millennia, of this lonely echoing land.

After two days stay at Inverary, we proceeded Southward over Glencroe, a black and dreary region, now made easily passable by a military road, which rises from either end of the glen by an acclivity not dangerously steep, but sufficiently laborious. In the middle, at the top of the hill, is a seat with this inscription, Rest, and be thankful. Stones were placed to mark the distances, which the inhabitants have taken away; resolved, they said, to have no new miles.

— Johnson

In the morning we rose to perambulate a city, which only history shews to have once flourished, and surveyed the ruins of ancient magnificence, of which even the ruins cannot long be visible, unless some care be taken to preserve them....

—Johnson

Author's Note

by Michael Ruetz

Before deciding on the famous "Journey to the Western Islands," undertaken in 1773, James Boswell informed Voltaire of the proposed venture: "He looked at me, as if I had talked of going to the North Pole, and said, 'You do not insist on my accompanying you?' – 'No sir' – 'Then I am very willing you should go.'" Perhaps nothing better illustrates the remoteness of this wild country, on the periphery of Europe, on the edge of our imagination, than the witty reply of France's greatest wit.

I wish to give the reader an explanation of my intention to visit and photograph Scotland – a Scotland, two centuries later, that is now as inviting as it was forbidding in Boswell's time.

The very title of the book gives a clue. "Scottish Symphony" is the name given by Felix Mendelssohn-Bartholdy to one of his most enduring works. For reasons very personal, his music has always been able to reach me, and I reasoned – and, as it turned out, correctly – that Scotland would attract me as it did him.

And even deeper than the way this music stirs me lies a personal affinity to James Boswell, the peripatetic, convivial, indefatigable traveler and companion-biographer of Samuel Johnson.

Boswell, of course, was a real Scot, had studied and taken his degree in Scotland. For more than a decade, he tried to prompt his revered "father" to undertake a trip to what then was considered as savage a country as the American colonies. When at last they made their journey, both wrote of their experiences: Johnson in *A Journey to the Western Islands of Scotland* and

Boswell in *The Journal of a Tour to the Hebrides*. Their manner of writing could not have been more different, for, while Johnson was looking at Scotland, Boswell was looking at Johnson look at Scotland. As critic Peter Levi writes: Boswell "unbuttons Johnson."

Johnson wrote of his experiences and reflections with the reserve of a man closing the book on a long and distinguished life. Boswell, on the other hand, wrote about Johnson doing just this, and showed little compunction about describing the great man's foibles. His book is, therefore, much livelier and more readable than Johnson's. Boswell's ironic humor makes his travel account one of the most entertaining in the English language.

It seems surprising that the scholarly Johnson, the cultural anthropologist, relied entirely on his memory, while the more easygoing Boswell kept a diary.

I believe that there is a close relationship between the making of photographs and the keeping of a diary. My own almost thirty years of diary writing, not leaving out a single day, explain in part my affinity to Boswell – I feel and see an invisible thread in our desire to portray our conception of reality in this way.

Boswell's account was first published in 1785. My affection for his journal led to the desire to commemorate the two hundredth anniversary of this important literary milestone with a photographic homage.

Scotland has a peculiar, harsh, tragic, melancholy beauty. Always changing. For me as a photographer it is a dream; the

After a very tedious ride, through what appeared to me the most gloomy and desolate country, I had ever beheld, we arrived, between seven and eight o'clock, at Moy, the seat of the Laird of Lochbuy.

— Boswell

When we had landed upon the sacred place, which, as long as I can remember, I had thought on with veneration, Dr. Johnson and I cordially embraced. We had long talked of visiting Icolmkill....

— Boswell

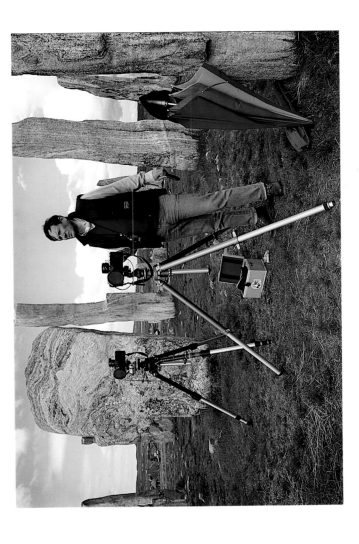

short exposure stops motion and allows us to slice unforgettable moments: the low-hanging clouds of the Highlands, the mysterious deep of its lochs and inlets. The ever-present dampness permeates our rain-slickers and makes its way into our reflections. The wind in Scotland, wailing and sighing, the ever-moving clouds, the short patches of blue sky, the emptiness of the countryside – such moments are impossible to capture elsewhere on this blue planet.

Scotland today is – just by virtue of its ever-changing clouds – different from yesterday, let alone two hundred years ago. However, I have tried to capture the Scotland that those travelers saw in its unadulterated state, and often that took me farther afield than their well-known journey through the glens and straths and lochs and towns. The reader of this book will find no people in the photographs, only some of the artifices that people have made for the past thousand or more years: castles, stone walls and churches – in short, man's things – next to God's things, seaweed, rocks, and clouds, tell us most about the Scotland of two centuries ago.

Luckily enough for me, I have chosen a profession which affords me the possibility of combining pleasure with work. Occasional inclement weather does not necessarily disturb my concentration or diminish my zeal. Making the photograph of Dunnottar Castle (Page 40), for example, required my returning several times and enduring a violent snowstorm. I remember standing on a rock opposite the castle for seven hours, shielding myself from the snow, and warming myself with a little Laphroaigh. Indispensable tools were my two trusty umbrellas.

* * *

All the photographs reproduced here were made outside the general tourist season in a series of three trips from November 1983 to late May 1984. During that time I drove approximately 13,000 miles and shot 550 rolls of film. For such a book, that might seem but a short time and as yet too few pictures. I must admit that, had I been able to, I would have spent several years in the lonely reaches of the Scottish Highlands and the Hebridean Isles.

Acknowledgments

There are many to whom I wish to offer thanks. It is with warmest appreciation and gratitude that I acknowledge Arthur H. Thornhill, Jr., and John Maclaurin, for their enthusiastic receptiveness to the project, and Terry Reece Hackford and Carl Zahn for their sensitivity to my work and the care that they devoted to create this volume. For their encouragement and support, I am also indebted to Nancy Robins and the staff of New York Graphic Society Books/Little, Brown and Company, and to Ingrid T. Schick, Helmut Penzlien, Michael S. Cullen, Marita Kankowski, and Margot Klingsporn.

I reserve my deepest thanks and respect for the people of Scotland. Perhaps because of the discovery of my own Celtic origins, my stay there felt like a homecoming. In my travels throughout the country, I did not experience even one moment of unkindness or unhappiness.

Michael Ruetz
Villa Massimo, Rome
April 1985

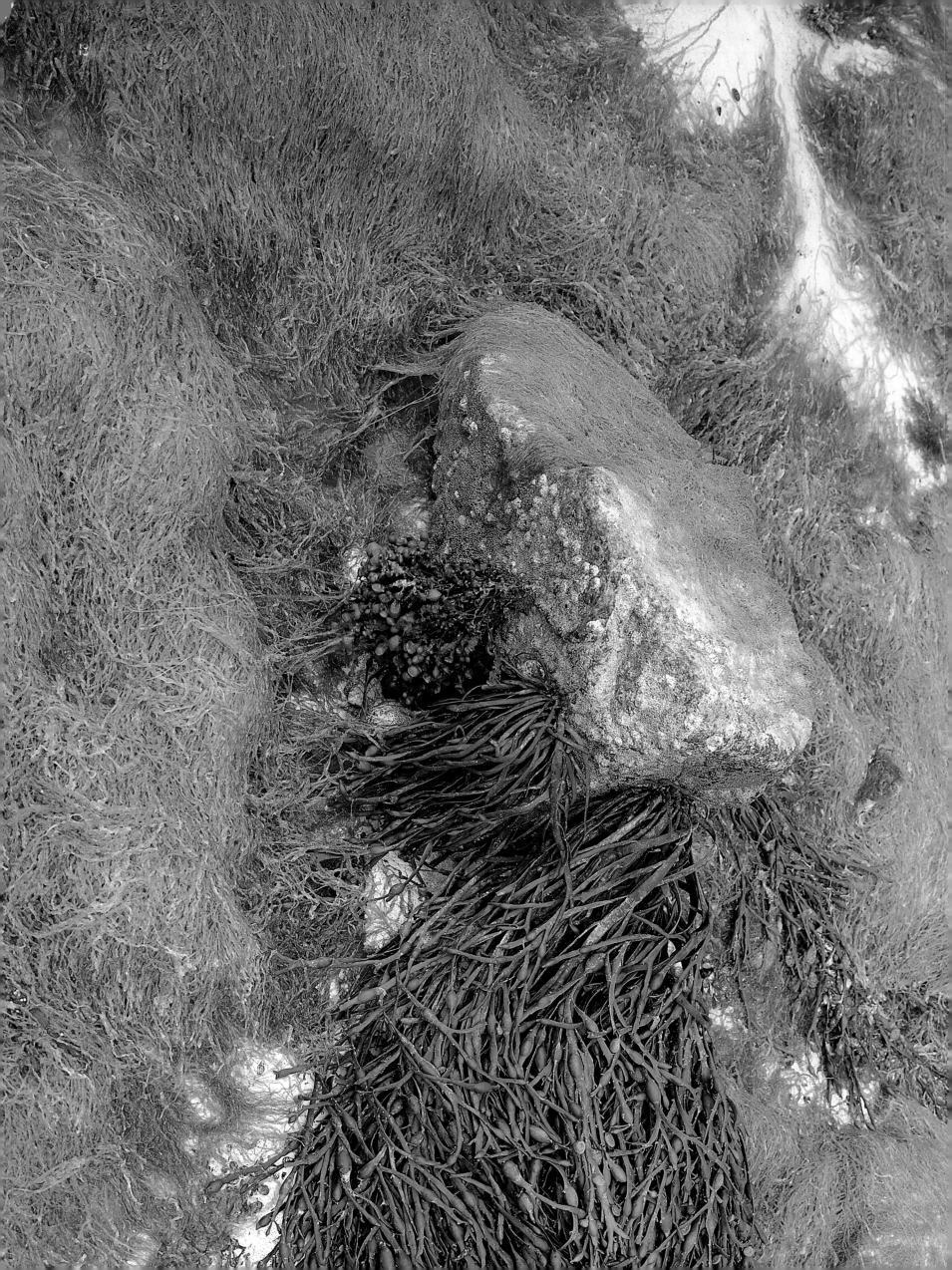

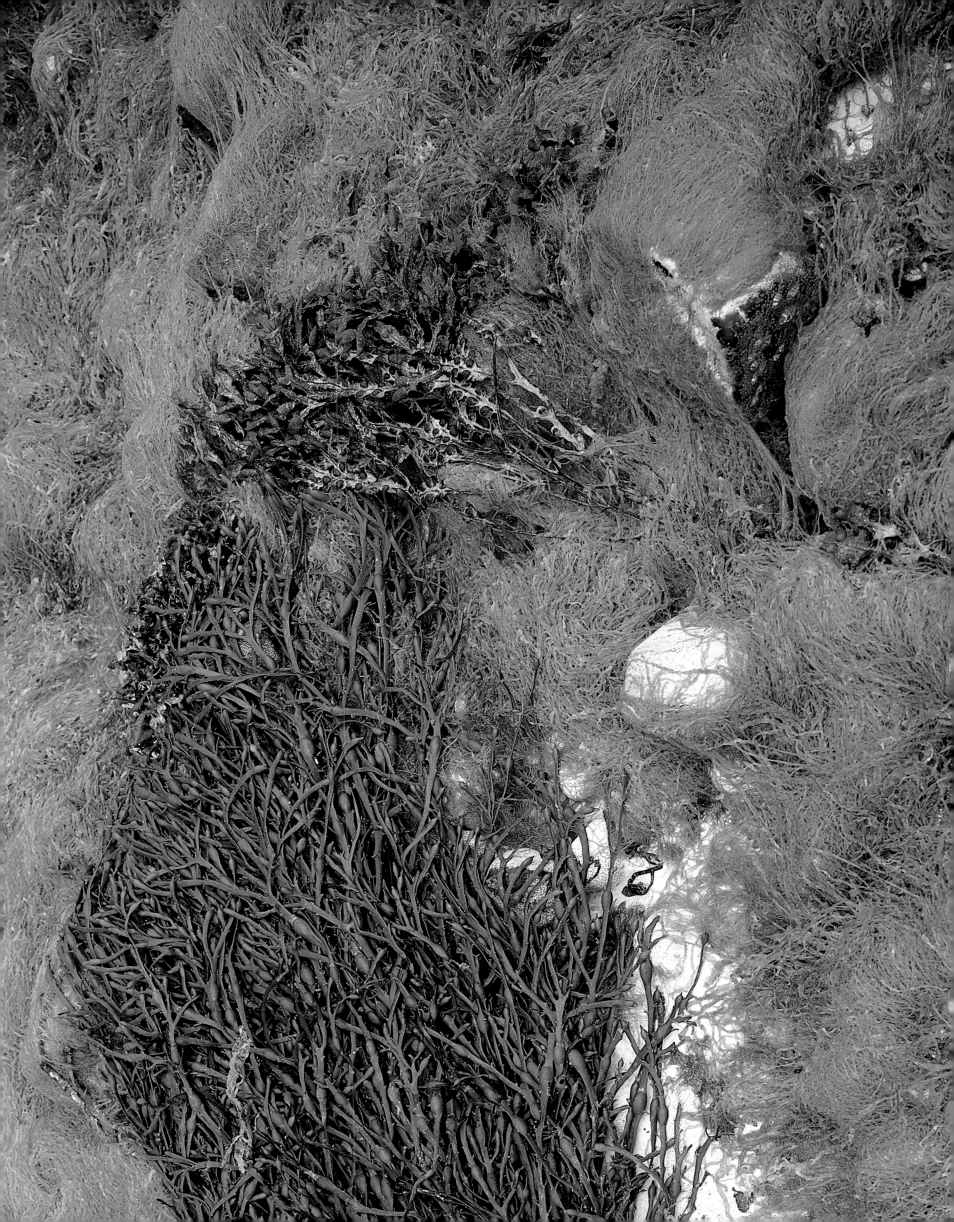

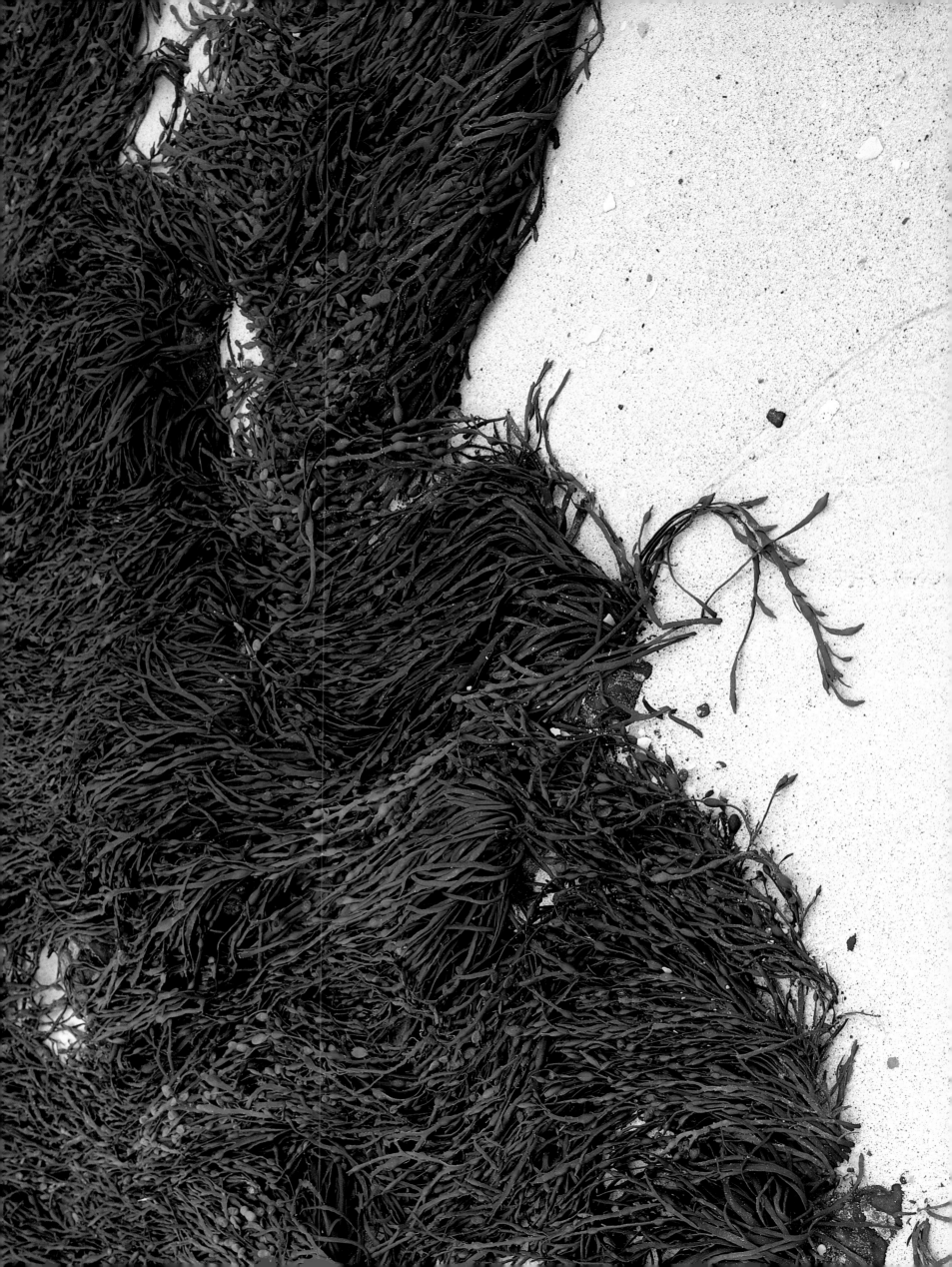

The night came on while we had yet a great part of the way to go, though not so dark, but that we could discern the cataracts which poured down the hills, on one side, and fell into one general channel that ran with great violence on the other. The wind was loud, the rain was heavy, and the whistling of the blast, the fall of the shower, the rush of the cataracts, and the roar of the torrent, made a nobler chorus of the rough musick of nature than it had ever been my chance to hear before.
       – Johnson

The only fewel of the Islands is peat. Their wood is all consumed, and coal they have not yet found.
       – Johnson

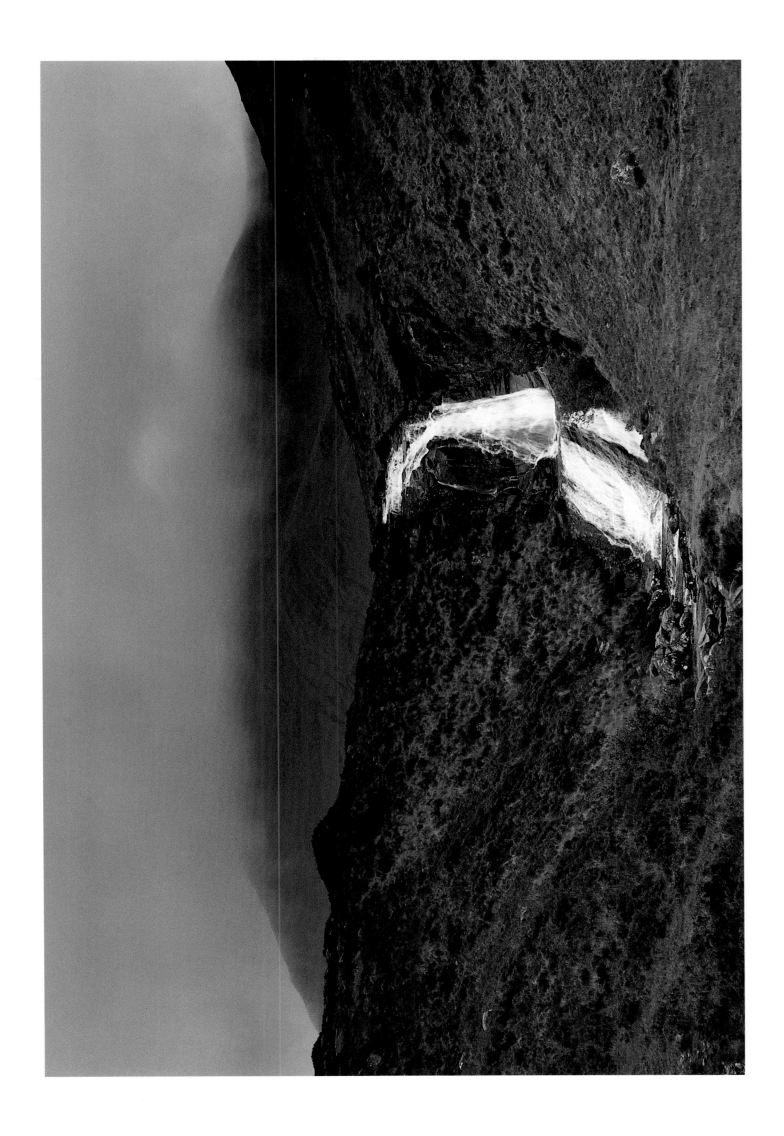

91 Glen Gairn, Grampian Mountains, Aberdeenshire

From the autumnal to the vernal equinox, a dry day is hardly known, except when the showers are suspended by a tempest. Under such skies can be expected no great exuberance of vegetation. Their winter overtakes their summer, and their harvest lies upon the ground drenched with rain.

– Johnson

92-93 Glen Gairn, Grampian Mountains, Aberdeenshire

94-95 Glen Gairn, Grampian Mountains, Aberdeenshire

97-99 Loch Tulla, Rannoch Moor, Argyllshire

100-101 Cloudy sky over pier at Salen, Isle of Mull

102-103 Lochan na h-Achlaise, Rannoch Moor, Argyllshire

104 Glen Croe, Argyllshire

After two days stay at Inverary we proceeded Southward over Glencroe, a black and dreary region, now made easily passable by a military road, which rises from either end of the glen by an acclivity not dangerously steep, but sufficiently laborious.

– Johnson

A castle in the Islands is only a single tower of three or four stories, of which the walls are sometimes eight or nine feet thick, with narrow windows, and close winding stairs of stone. The top rises in a cone, or pyramid of stone, encompassed by battlements.

– Johnson

I sat down on a bank, such as a writer of Romance might have delighted to feign. I had indeed no trees to whisper over my head, but a clear rivulet streamed at my feet. The day was calm, the air soft, and all was rudeness, silence, and solitude.

– Johnson

129 *Loch Garry, Perthshire*

130-131 *Loch nan Uamh, Inverness-shire*

132-133 *Caledonian pines, Loch Eil, Inverness-shire*

135-137 *Old Man of Storr, Isle of Skye*

In traveling even thus almost without light thro' naked solitude, when there is a guide whose conduct may be trusted, a mind not naturally too much disposed to fear, may preserve some degree of cheerfulness; but what must be the solicitude of him who should be wandering, among the craggs and hollows, benighted, ignorant, and alone?

– Johnson

138-139 *Loch Laggan, Glen Spean, Inverness-shire*

140-141 *Lone tree on Loch Lomond, Dumbartonshire*

The variety of sun and shade is here utterly unknown. There is no tree for either shelter or timber....A tree might be a show in Scotland as a horse in Venice.

– Johnson

142 *Stone wall near Sligachan, Isle of Skye*

Regions mountainous and wild, thinly-inhabited, and little cultivated, make a great part of the earth, and he that has never seen them, must live unacquainted with much of the face of nature, and with one of the great scenes of human existence.

— Johnson

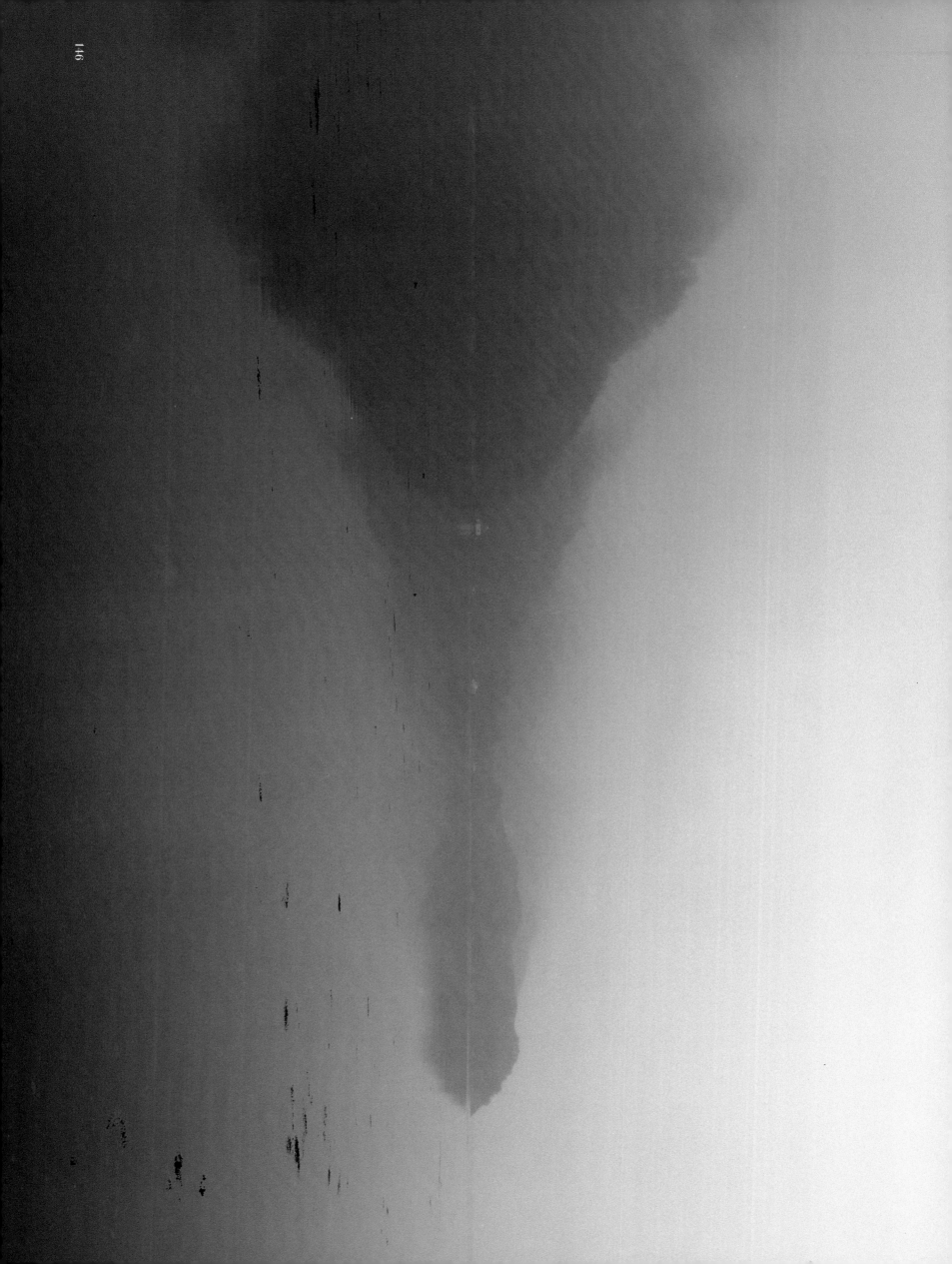

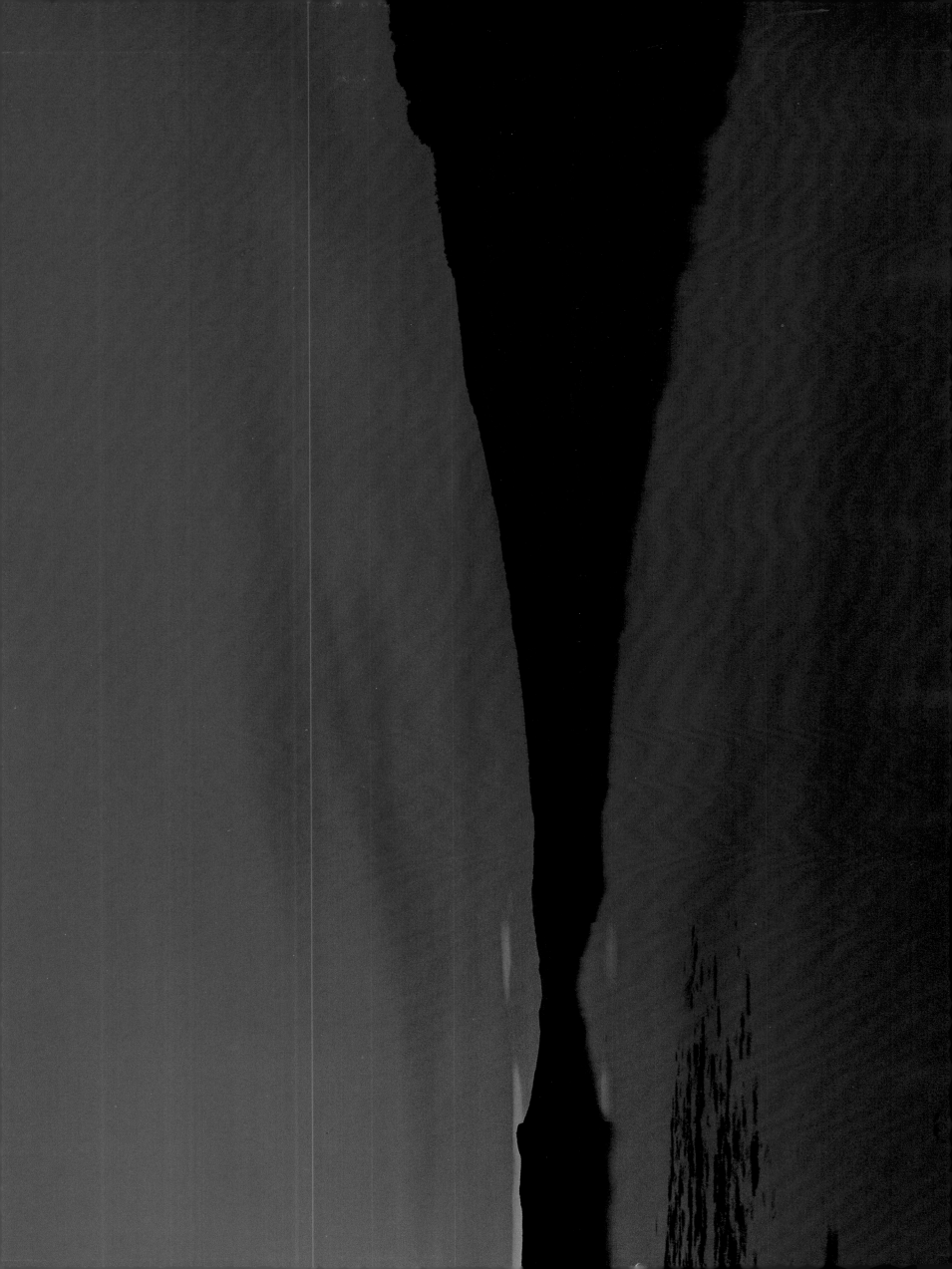

List of Plates

All quotations from James Boswell are drawn from The Journal of a Tour to the Hebrides with Samuel Johnson, LL.D., published by George Routledge & Sons, [1852]. The quotations from Samuel Johnson are drawn from A Journey to the Western Islands of Scotland, printed for W. Strahan & T. Cadell in the Strand, 1775 (first edition).

In the key that follows, the pages in Scottish Symphony are followed by references to the quotation source. The date of the diary entry is used for the Boswell quotations, and the page number in the first edition for the Johnson quotations: 12, 371 and October 21: 14, 348 and October 19: 19, October 3: 25-27, October 19: 30-31, 184: 32, October 19: 35, September 25: 36-37, 343-44: 42-43, August 30: 59, September 13: 60-61, 7: 65-67, 36: 70-71, 323-24: 75, 37: 88, 235: 91, 76: 104, 371: 108-09, 361: 124-25, 86-87, 135-37, 174: 140-41, 16: 154, 85-86.